MW00879218

This Journal Belongs To :

Date :

Made in the USA
Monee, IL
03 March 2022

92199812R00069